CODING YOUR PASSION™

USING COMPUTER SCIENCE IN MEDIA CAREERS

DON RAUF

Rosen YA™
New York

Published in 2020 by The Rosen Publishing Group, Inc.
29 East 21st Street, New York, NY 10010

First Edition

Library of Congress Cataloging-in-Publication Data

Names: Rauf, Don, author.
Title: Using computer science in media careers / Don Rauf.
Description: First edition. | New York : Rosen Publishing, 2020. | Series: Coding your passion | Includes bibliographical references and index. | Audience: Grades: 7–12.
Identifiers: LCCN 2018043390| ISBN 9781508187226 (library bound) | ISBN 9781508187219 (pbk.)
Subjects: LCSH: Mass media—Vocational guidance—Juvenile literature. | Computer science—Vocational guidance—Juvenile literature. | Mass media and technology—Juvenile literature.
Classification: LCC P91.6 .R38 2020 | DDC 302.23023—dc23
LC record available at https://lccn.loc.gov/2018043390

Manufactured in the United States of America

CONTENTS

INTRODUCTION

How do you get your news and information about the world? You may listen to a podcast or stream a news program on your phone. You may follow several publications or blogs. Or you may watch a documentary or read books about important current affairs. All these ways of communicating information to a large number of people are known collectively as the media. And today there are more types of media than ever before. We're surrounded by information wherever we go. Information is not only on our portable devices, but bombarding us on screens in elevators, taxis, and even at the gas pump.

Media jobs in television, film, radio, and online can all offer exciting opportunities for those who care about ideas and information and presenting them to the general public. Joan Grossman is an independent filmmaker who teaches video production at the Middlebury College School of the Environment in Vermont and China. She has also produced programming for public radio and made multimedia installations for museums and galleries internationally that expand the documentary form. Grossman always had a strong interest in journalism. When she studied the subject at Northwestern University Medill School of Journalism in Chicago, she realized that media could have many forms. "When we use the term 'the media,' people are thinking of everything from print

Today, people get their news from all sorts of devices, often in quick short doses from their smartphones and other handheld devices.

journalism to films and video to internet content—it's all part of our mass media system," she said in an interview for this book. "Today, it's not just a few networks broadcasting to many but many entities distributing information to the public."

This new media landscape grew with the help of the computer. When images and sounds could be digitized and uploaded to a computer, they became easier to capture, edit, and distribute. Technology paved the way for a tsunami of information from an endless number of sources. While the world of media is certainly a creative one, success in this field requires a strong knowledge of computer science. "Computers are playing a bigger and bigger role in media and this role is evolving all the time," said Grossman.

Almost all media jobs today require computer skills, and the more you have, the more valuable and attractive you may be to employers. Advanced computer skills can mean more earning potential as well. Software, hardware, and coding are essential components in media, even in areas that are not always associated with high tech—such as book publishing and newspaper journalism. Even if you don't master coding and more complex skills, some computer talent is a must in the media universe.

Many schools today include science, technology, engineering, and mathematics (STEM) in their curricula. All these subjects can help students better understand computers and the principles on which they operate. Many educators have added another more creative element to this mix and advocate for a curriculum called STEAM (science, technology, engineering, art, and mathematics). STEAM proponents believe in encouraging creative thinking and innovation, and they see art as a means of achieving that. Certainly, these are qualities needed in the media world today. While all STEAM-related knowledge is helpful, students may still need to take an extra step and pursue specific computer training if their school doesn't offer such courses.

Microsoft founder Bill Gates has stressed how important computers are in all our lives today and why learning how they work can be advantageous: "I think it's fair to say that personal computers have become the most empowering tool we've ever created. They're tools of communication, they're tools of creativity, and they can be shaped by their user."

CHAPTER ONE

MEDIA GOES DIGITAL

Media careers offer many interesting, challenging, and creative opportunities. Those entering the media field today know that computers and the internet have changed everything. While traditional print and broadcast media have not gone away, they have had to adapt to survive by embracing technology and offering their content digitally. The use of the internet and digital technology for mass communication has been dubbed new media. Consumers today are much more likely to get their news through Facebook and Google than a newspaper or the six o'clock news, as many people used to.

The media businesses that have survived and thrived have embraced change and stayed up to date with current trends. In an article in Medium, Jamie Gavin, managing director of inPress Online, a media agency that helps businesses with media strategies, said that publishers have had to adapt by making their content shorter, shareable, and relevant for multiple formats.

Currently, about two-thirds of Americans report that they get at least some of their news on social media such as Facebook.

COMPUTER SKILLS ARE A MUST

By fully embracing new media, Michael Rosenblum established a very successful career. He started in TV news, where segments were filmed using a crew, cameraman, producer, and reporter, but he saw that quality personalized TV journalism could be made by one person with one small video camera, who films his or her own footage of news in the making and edits it using software on a computer. He showed many media outlets how to use this cost-saving idea. For example,

Rosenblum took the concept to Current TV, which he founded with Al Gore. Overall, he has produced more than 8,000 hours of content using this one-person-with-a-camera method. To teach others, he established the online video/TV/film school TheVJ.com.

To succeed in the media world today, Rosenblum stresses that computer skills are a must. "Television, film, and video production today are 100 percent computer skills," said Rosenblum in an interview for this book. "We shoot all of our video on phones now. The video is a digital file. The editing is done on a computer, and the distribution is done online. It is a 100 percent computer-based industry. The more skills you have the better off."

In *Forbes* magazine, writer Mike Elgan calls young adults today "digital natives," meaning people born in the age of digital technology. He recognizes that they are using computers more than previous generations, but they "don't know what's going on under the hood" because using a computer doesn't take as much knowledge and skill as it once did. He said that they are often comfortable with solving problems with an app or an internet-based service, but they need to know how to build their own creative solutions and have a better understanding of computers.

Elgan encourages students to pursue more computer education: "Software development should become a core part of public education, required of all students. By the time kids graduate from high school, they should be able to build a PC, troubleshoot networking issues, and at the very least be able to build and manage a moderately complex Web site."

Many young people get their media through computers, smartphones, and tablets. They could benefit from learning the software and technology that make them work.

While this may seem like a lot or even too much to some, the fact is that media businesses need employees who understand computing, and the more knowledge, the better.

WORKING AS A MEDIA SOFTWARE DEVELOPER

Software developers are known as problem solvers who use programming languages to create new products and services. Their code is behind the apps and programs that make computers do the various tasks they are asked to perform. While developers know how to write code, they often conceive the bigger picture on a project and hand off the coding to computer programmers.

Developers determine user needs, map out the goals, create diagrams and maps for coders to follow, and possibly teach the programmers about the code that specifically needs to be written for the project. Software developer Michal Franc writes on his website: "From my experience I can say, that this is one of the best jobs someone can do. It is creative, demanding and extremely rewarding plus it has an awesome community with friendly and intelligent people."

The *Washington Post* has recognized the need for journalists who understand software, so the company supports an educational program to inspire talented developers to move into media and journalism. The *Post*'s computer engineering team works in partnership with the company's award-winning newsroom to develop innovative products to improve the reader experience. Software developers work alongside reporters and editors in the newsroom to foster greater collaboration.

HackerRank.com is an online service where millions of developers practice code, prepare for interviews, and get hired. In an article in *The Inquirer*, Ritika Trikha, a researcher with HackerRank.com, said that the most in-demand computer languages are Java, Python, C, and C++. "These four fundamental pillars are what make up the majority of businesses' code," said Trikha in the article.

Note that computer programmer is another career that is closely related to software developer. If you compared the computer world to the auto industry, you could say the software developers design the cars, but the programmers put them together. The programmers—also called coders—are those who write the code that makes the software work. Part of the job is testing.

The Bureau of Labor Statistics (BLS) says that professionals in this field typically have a bachelor's degree in computer science and a strong background in programming. The BLS predicts that job growth for software developers will be very strong through at least 2026. Although programmers continue to be in demand on the job market, the BLS indicates that opportunities for programmers are expected to decline slightly through 2026 because this job can be outsourced to programmers around the globe.

WORKING AS AN INTERACTIVE MEDIA DESIGNER

Eye-catching design never goes out of style, but the graphic designers of today can tap into more opportunities if they hone interactive media skills. These graphic designers find opportunities in almost every area of media, from publishing to television to public relations. They work to make interfaces on websites and mobile phones that not only look good but that are easy and interesting for customers to use. They learn how to incorporate options that allow users to swipe, tap, click, and input information, such as passwords and credit card numbers.

Animation is often an element in interactive media, and many software packages are now available to bring moving 2D and 3D images to customer computers and smartphones. OpenToonz, for example, is a popular 2D animation software. Autodesk 3ds Max, iClone, and Aladdin 4D are among the top programs for handling 3D animation. Because their creations are often incorporated into websites, these designers may learn HTML, CSS, and JavaScript. CSS and JavaScript are used to create online animations.

Many interactive media designers also have an understanding of apps and application software. When Nastasha Tan wrote about her work as an interaction designer on Ideo.com, she explained that she used two computer screens to design apps. On one screen, she used Sketch software to design the screens of an app and then on another screen, she displayed a Google Doc that provided a work-in-progress narrative, showing her what'd been done and what tasks had yet to be completed.

Layout, graphics, and production design for advertisements, brochures, websites, magazines, and corporate reports are all done on computers using programs such as Adobe Photoshop, Adobe Illustrator, Adobe InDesign, and CorelDraw Graphics Suite.

This career generally requires a four-year degree in graphic design, interactive media design, or art-related study. BLS predicts the opportunities will grow through 2026, but they will be slower than average.

UNDERSTANDING THE NUTS AND BOLTS...OR BITS AND BYTES

For those with little or no knowledge of computers, programs operate on a binary language. While most of us are accustomed to the decimal system based on numerals 1 through 9, the binary system operates on 0s and 1s.

Binary is known as the language of computers. Computers complete tasks through the use of

(continued on the next page)

Computers and digital devices use the binary system of 0s and 1s to store and manipulate data. The 0s and 1s indicate whether transistors in a computer are turned on or off.

(continued from the previous page)

transistors, tiny switches that trigger electric signals. The switches are in either of two binary states—0 or 1, indicating either on or off. Binary code is the language that tells the computer which switches to turn on and which switches to turn off.

If all code were written in binary, it would take an impossible amount of time to get the billions of 0s and 1s properly constructed. Computer scientists, fortunately, figured out a way to write computer languages, such as Java, that can tell a computer what to do. The programming language gets translated into a binary machine code, which the computer can read and execute.

Using programming languages, professionals create software (the programs that tell a computer how to operate). The devices and the physical components on which the software operates are called hardware.

LEARNING THE LANGUAGE OF COMPUTERS

Although you don't need to learn how to code to land a job in media, some basic coding knowledge can make a job candidate more hirable. Apple cofounder Steve Jobs once said, "I think everybody in this country should learn how to program a computer because it teaches you how to think."

Software developers are the creative brains behind the programs that let computers perform different tasks, such as running a video on screen or making apps for mobile devices.

Here are a few of the top programming languages that may help in a media career.

C: C was mainly designed as a system programming language and is one of the oldest and most popular. Microsoft Windows was developed mostly in C. It is also the language used in many electronics—from cell phones to alarm clocks.

C++: A highly popular and versatile coding language, C++ was conceived in 1979 and remains a mainstay for software developers everywhere. It's known to handle complex tasks and performs them quickly.

CSS (Cascading Style Sheets): CSS are instructions that style the web pages, defining how they should look in terms of fonts and colors. These sheets tell the computer or mobile browser how content should look to the user. CSS define layout, position, alignment, height, width, typefaces, borders, and more.

HTML (Hypertext Markup Language): This is the language at the foundation for building Web pages. All the graphics and information that you see on web pages are structured using HTML. HTML allows a person to design a web page so it can present text, images, and links to other web pages, videos, interactive forms, and more. A web page is a type of user interface (UI), the visual element on a screen that the user interacts with.

Java: Ranked as the most popular programming language, Java is often used on the server side (rather than the client, or user, side) to handle a variety of tasks from processing requests to delivering data. Java has been the official language for app development for Android devices.

JavaScript: Often used along with HTML in creating web pages, JavaScript is used to make interactive features. These features may be navigation toggles (such as menu buttons and dropdown screens, interactive maps, and simple online games).

Python: Known to be easy to use and learn, Python is a practical choice for a range of programming work. It can be very efficient for processing a high volume of data.

SQL (Structured Query Language): This language is especially good for storing, manipulating, and querying data stored in databases. Because it is very practical in handling huge amounts of information, organizations dealing with lots of customers find it very useful.

CHAPTER TWO

LIGHTS, CAMERA, CODING: COMPUTER SCIENCE IN TELEVISION AND FILM

Motion pictures have come a long way since 1888 when French inventor Louis le Prince filmed people walking around a garden. "The Roundhay Garden Scene" is said to be the oldest surviving film in existence, and if you have two seconds to spare, you can view it on YouTube.

Just as Le Prince's video was an innovation in media for its time, YouTube has been one of the major media innovations of our time. YouTube was born in the spring of 2005, and now over a billion people upload and watch videos via this platform. The technology rose out of the scientific advancement of digital photography and film.

The first digital video technology arrived on the scene in 1995, according to *Electronic Component News*, when Panasonic and Sony began selling the first digital video camcorders. After the first digital still photo camera came out in the 1970s, it was only a matter of time before digital film and video would arrive.

Digital technology paved the way for YouTube. For over a decade, the technology has allowed virtually anyone to post videos online.

Digital formats have been money savers because it was much more expensive to take repeated shots on film or tape. The digital platform made editing easier as well. When digital segments could be easily transferred to a computer, film editing went from manually slicing frames on celluloid or transferring desired video segments from one video to another to cutting and pasting film segments together on a computer screen by clicking and dragging. With the right software, a difficult process was now much less labor intensive.

"New digital technologies opened up all kinds of possibilities and transformed the media field to one that requires comfort with computers," said independent filmmaker Joan Grossman in an interview for this book. "If you're not really comfortable with computers nowadays, it's not a field you can excel in."

SHOWING WORKS TO THE WORLD

The new digital technology also makes it easy for film and video makers to upload their work to online

IN THE CLOUD

Besides using computers to upload and manage content on the internet, filmmakers are also using cloud-based tools. The cloud is basically a term used for internet-based computing. When it comes to storage, information resides on a server rather than on a person's computer or external hard drive. Then that data can be accessed and easily shared through an online connection. Film and video makers can back up large files to the cloud to keep them protected. They can also download and use software from the cloud. Adobe sells its software this way. Since it's cloud based, you're not buying the software as a physical product. You're subscribing to it and accessing it off the cloud. That way, you always have a current version.

services such as YouTube, where they can share their production with the world. Computers and the internet have made it so that a lot of content can be produced and presented to the world. Grossman said that a popular form of media now is the short film and video. "Short-form videos are everywhere," she said. "Organizations are using them to get their messages out, they are also popular as entertainment—as used in web series, for example."

Films and videos can be streamed on demand to phones, web pages, or directly into a consumer's home television set. Again, coding makes it all work. (Roku streaming players rely on a proprietary computer language called BrightScript with XML, and Amazon

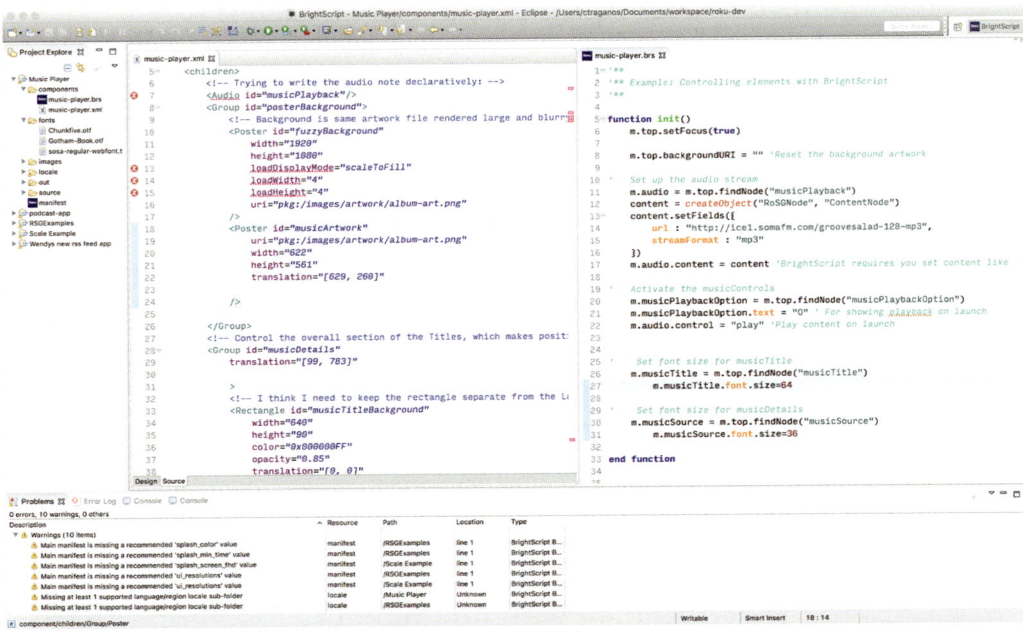

Devices like the Roku streaming player run on very powerful and detailed computer code.

Fire TV relies on technology using Android OS, which is based on Java and XML.)

LIFE AS A DIGITAL FILM EDITOR

Because technology has made cameras and computers more affordable, more people interested in directing television and film have started to learn about filmmaking and create their own work.

Nathan Leatherman, a student in the television production program at Murray State University in Kentucky, is not only a digital filmmaker but also a digital film editor. One of the projects he shot and edited was a short documentary about students who visited Korea. After writing scripts with word processing software, Leatherman films on a portable DSLR (digital single lens reflex camera) and then transfers all the files to his computer, where he can edit and manipulate the footage. Adjusting the film or video after shooting is called postproduction. Before piecing together all the segments into a final end product, the digital editor may make an outline of all the scenes that were filmed to have a guide to refer to.

One of the most popular film editing software packages is Adobe Creative Suite. The package includes Adobe Premiere Pro for video editing. Apple makes another popular film editing tool called Final Cut Pro. Users familiar with editing software can process the scenes they have filmed—stringing them together in the order they wish, cutting out specific

Software such as Adobe Premiere Pro (www.adobe.com) gives users the tools to make professional-looking videos on their home computers.

sections, manipulating the images, and adjusting the sound. The software—built on lines and lines of code—does the hard work by carrying out the instructions that the film editor gives. Adobe Premiere Pro was built mainly using C++ computer language.

Nathan Leatherman said that he uses a type of coding with Adobe After Effects, which is a software application for creating motion graphics and special effects used in video. A film editor can animate a title across a screen or build a 3D world. After Effects provides a feature called Expressions. Expressions are basically ways to manipulate filmed images using code. The After Effects' Expressions language is based on the programming language JavaScript. "Expressions is code that lets you tell After Effects to do certain things," Leatherman said in an interview for this book. "It gives you greater control than just clicking provided boxes and moving sliders on the screen." Schoolofmotion.com gives a great tutorial showing how to apply Expressions to make the hands of a clock rotate at a specific rate. Film editors may also incorporate voice-over and music and assure that dialogue is syncing up with the characters on screen.

Leatherman notes that a knowledge of HTML coding has also helped him maintain his web page, where he presents samples of his video work. He has used coding to adjust web page dimensions and image resolution. "I have at least a basic understanding of the coding world," he said. "Although most people don't need to worry about coding, it's good to know how things work behind the tools you are using."

Digital film and video editors make commercials, corporate training videos, feature films, music videos, and television programs. The Bureau of Labor Statistics says that the future is promising in terms of employment opportunities, with an 11 percent increase in job growth between 2014 and 2024.

WORKING AS A VISUAL EFFECTS (VFX) ARTIST

Computer programming provides film and television productions with a wide range of special effects and almost anything that can be imagined can be brought to life on the screen. Computer-generated imagery (CGI) has created everything from explosions to spaceships to flying monsters.

Popular programs for special effects include After Effects, Shakes, Renderman, and Houdini. Visual effects artists may also storyboard the action for a film using software, such as StudioBinder, Moviestorm, and FrameForge, that allows the user to visually outline the scenes in film or video production. Sometimes, they use their computers for reference work to accurately re-create creatures such as

Motion capture technology records the movements of an actor and translates them to a digital character.

dinosaurs, megasharks, rocket ships, the *Titanic*, or the surface of a distant planet. Special effects can enhance documentaries, scientific programs, and television news segments.

Neil Huxley has worked as a VFX designer and an art director on major motion pictures such as *Avatar* and *The Watchmen*, and he has brought his talents to a documentary on East London boxer Jimmy Flint. He got his start combining design and visual effects by making a title sequence for the movie *Salem's Lot*.

When asked what it takes to get into VFX design in an interview in Yokedesign.com, Huxley said, "It's a cliché and I find myself repeating this a lot, but it's all about hard work and drive. How badly do you want it? Apply yourself, build a killer reel, apply to companies you would love to work for and you will get a foot in the door."

To gain experience with industry-standard software, those pursuing this career typically study animation, computer graphics, or graphic design at college. Some special effects studios will offer training programs. A few schools that are known for their VFX training are Gnomon School of Visual Effects, Games, and Animation in Los Angeles; Lost Boy Studios in Vancouver, British Columbia; and Ringling College of Art and Design in Sarasota, Florida. Note also that computer animation is a closely related field that requires many of the same skills and software knowledge. The Bureau of Labor Statistics estimates job growth at 6 percent between 2014 and 2024.

WORKING AS A BROADCAST TECHNICIAN

Broadcast technicians set up, operate, and maintain the electronic equipment used to transmit radio and television programs. The electronic controls they adjust regulate the color, contrast, sound, and sharpness of the images being broadcast. On a news program, they are the ones switching between the live broadcast and prerecorded segments.

Some technicians use Caliope broadcast automation software, which provides a means for storing, viewing, and editing, but also automates the scheduling process. They often work irregular shifts because broadcasting goes around the clock.

While most of the work is indoors, they do get outside often to broadcast "remotes," or segments filmed on location, and setting up broadcast equipment such as antennas can be physically demanding at times.

A high school diploma along with on-the-job training is often enough to get started in this field. Students can get experience volunteering at a college television or radio station. A radio and television technician degree from a community college or technical school can provide a solid base of knowledge. They may earn a degree in degree in computer networking, broadcast technology, or electronics. The US Bureau of Labor Statistics projected a 7 percent growth in opportunities for broadcast technicians between 2014 and 2024.

CHAPTER THREE

ON THE AIR: COMPUTER SCIENCE IN RADIO

Although he admits that he is no computer expert, radio producer and podcast host Trey Kay said that no one in radio production today could do his or her job without some understanding of computers. For more than two decades, Trey Kay has been producing radio news features for public radio programs such as *This American Life*, *Studio 360*, *Morning Edition*, and *Marketplace*. His latest job is as the host and creator of *Us & Them*, a podcast on West Virginia Public Broadcasting and PRX (the Public Radio Exchange).

As a popular podcast, *Us & Them* is a good example of how computer technology has changed the medium of radio. Computers opened up a new door to how we listen to news, commentary, and real-life stories. Podcasts are a prime example of this.

Podcasts are downloadable audio programs on a variety of subjects. With the right technology, anyone can make podcasts on his or her home computer and reach a wide range of listeners.

DIGITAL TOOLS OF THE TRADE

To keep up with producing a podcast twice a month, Trey Kay relies on an arsenal of digital tools. He records all his audio as digital files using recorders made by Zoom, Tascam, and Sony. Then, he takes that raw audio and transfers it over to a hard drive or computer. Some of his portable recorders use tiny SD (Secure Digital) cards to provide high-capacity memory.

When he started in the business, he would record audio onto mini disks or DAT tape, and then he would

Top-quality recorders, such as those made by Zoom, Sony, and Tascam, can allow a homemade podcast to sound like a professional radio broadcast.

have to use a program to download the audio into his computer in real time. So two hours of conversation would take two hours to download. Modern software makes that process almost instantaneous. Kay will have volumes of audio recorded in a wav file format. When he connects his recorder to the computer, it's a simple drag-and-drop process to move the audio files. Because he usually has so much material, he depends on external hard drives to store files.

Kay has also found that his iPhone can be a great tool for recording notes that he can later have transcribed for a project and sometimes for recording when he doesn't have his high-end gear. Various apps, such as Temi and Trint, also provide low-cost transcription. Some services that churn out computer-generated transcripts are surprisingly accurate, and they complete the task in less time than the actual recording length.

HOW TO CREATE YOUR OWN PODCAST

Almost anyone with a good concept and some simple computer equipment can launch his or her own podcast. Here are a few basic steps:

1. **Define your show. What will you be talking about? What is the theme of your program? How will it stand out from other shows? Will there be guests? How will the show be organized?**

(continued on the next page)

(continued from the previous page)

2. **Get a good microphone.** Podcasts have to be high quality to succeed. That means investing in equipment. An Audio-Technica AT2020 is a popular and economical podcasting microphone.
3. **Get the right software.** Zencastr is an example of high-quality podcasting software that allows you a professional level of recording and editing. Auphonic is another option worth checking out. Garageband, Logic Pro, and Adobe Audition are all solid choices for recording, editing, and adjusting recording quality.
4. **Record your podcast.** Write out your plan for a show and record all the audio. You can record much more than you need and then edit it down later—most podcasts are no longer than sixty minutes and thirty to forty-five minutes is ideal.
5. **Choose a hosting/streaming service.** When a podcast is ready for distribution, it needs to be uploaded in an MP3 form to a podcast host. Some of the top hosting services are Buzzsprout, Libsyn, Blubrry, Podbean, and Pod.ad. The listeners stream the show via iTunes, Stitcher, Google Play, and TuneIn, among others.
6. **Create a website for your podcast.** A website dedicated to your podcast helps to promote your show and gives fans a place to stay in touch, ask questions, stay up-to-date, share information, and build community.

WRANGLING INFORMATION

One of Kay's biggest concerns is losing valuable audio. Soon after he downloads it, he makes sure to send his files to three editors who work on the show. That way he knows there will be at least three other copies of the audio. The files are usually too big to send via normal email, so Kay uses a file transfer service, such as WeTransfer.com or WeSendIt.com. Sometimes, he places files on Dropbox, which is a file hosting service. Dropbox is an example of the current cloud technology. He also sends his recordings to a transcriber. With a full written version of his material, he can readily mark up which segments he wants to use.

In his line of work, Kay also has to read a lot of material to get a fuller grasp of subject matter. Because he is dyslexic, he relies on his computer to help him. His Apple computer provides a function under its preferences that lets him highlight text that can than be read back to him as he reads.

"That's been a groundbreaking tool for me," said Kay. "Reading a *New Yorker* article could normally take me a day to read. But if I need to read quickly under pressure, this function helps me get through the material. The way I describe it is like a rope that pulls me along a little. It helps me read faster and process material."

SOFTWARE FOR AUDIO STORYTELLING

Kay pieces together his audio with software called Pro Tools. Many professional recording studios and home recorders rely on Pro Tools for mixing music, because it gives the ability to have many different tracks dedicated to different audio in a song. Just as a recording studio will devote one track to vocals, one track to guitar, one track to bass, and so on, Kay designates different tracks for his needs. One is devoted to the narration of the story where he is talking to the audience. Other tracks are assigned for his "actualities," or "acts" for short. In radio broadcast journalism, actualities are also known as newsmaker sound bites (or soundbytes). These are the words that other people say.

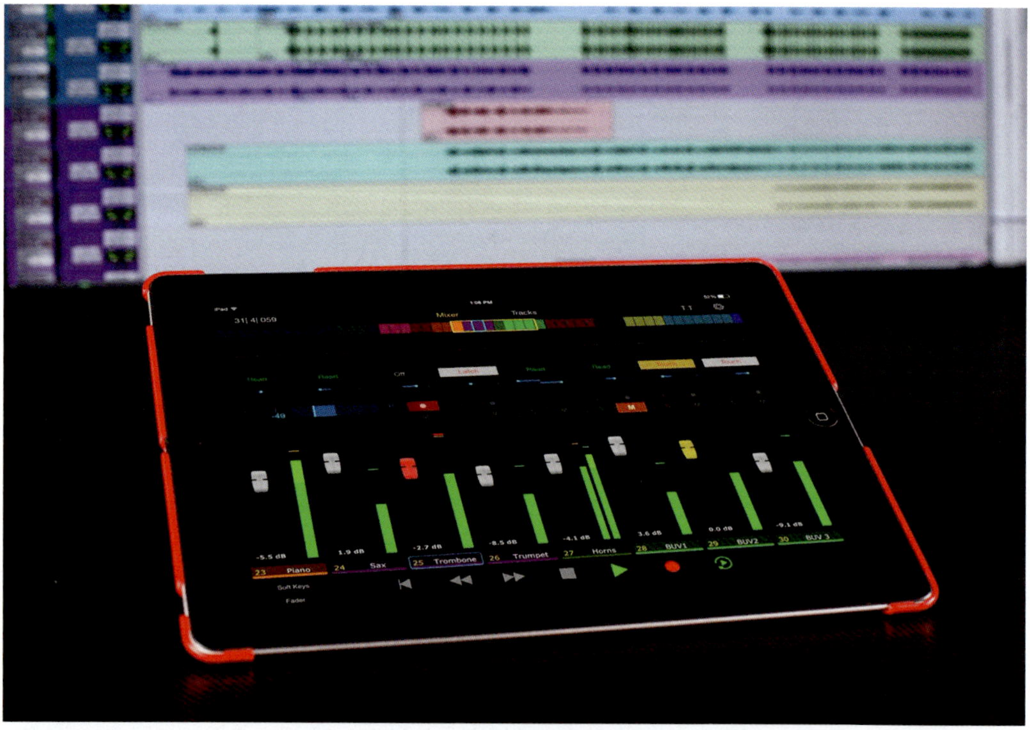

The digital audio workstation Pro Tools, developed by Avid Technology, helps audio engineers mix sounds on different tracks to create their final audio program.

To make the listener feel like he or she is at the actual location, Kay has a track for ambient sound. When he was interviewing farmers in Arkansas, he got out in the field and recorded just the sounds of farm equipment running. "I use tracks like this as my sound design to give the listener a feeling of what it's like to be in the place where the person I'm interviewing lives or works," he said.

Often in radio journalism, a script will be generated indicating the length of each audio segment. NPR tracks and modifies stories with software called NewsFlex, and employees work on projects using the software Slack, which is a collaboration hub where the people you need, the information you share, and the tools you use come together to get things done.

Kay says that different software is available for mixing audio but having experience in one makes it easier to use any of them. "Computers and digital editing software are similar to car rentals," said Kay. "The cars may be different, but you know where all the functions and parts are so you can operate different types."

When Kay has put together a finished product, he sends it to an audio engineer, who adjusts the sound to a level that is broadcast quality. Then, via his computer, he uploads his entire program to a couple of the services that distribute podcasts so listeners can download the show to their devices.

Radio stations are adapting to the computer era by offering their own podcasts and streaming their broadcasts over the internet so they can be heard anywhere in the world. Websites show how just about

Podcasts have become so popular that many broadcast radio and television stations have jumped into the game and begun making their own.

anyone can start their own internet radio station and "broadcast" from home.

WORKING AS AN AUDIO EDITOR/ENGINEER

Using editing software, audio editors or engineers take recordings and create a variety of audio stories, news items, and sound bites to be broadcast or played via podcast. They may occasionally travel to locations to help set up and operate recording equipment. Using audio software such as Adobe Audition, Pro Tools, and Audacity, they may improve sound quality and add in sound effects. In general, their role is to support a producer who is creating or orchestrating the content.

"At Sound Lounge (an audio postproduction company), we use Pro Tools as a digital audio workstation (DAW) for all the audio work," wrote audio engineer Justin Matley online. "Knowing the software well enough to accomplish your sonic goals is important."

The BLS states that audio and video equipment technicians, as well as sound engineering technicians, typically need a postsecondary nondegree award or certificate to demonstrate skill competency. The Society of Broadcast Engineers offers eight broadcast engineering certifications. Also, check out InfoComm International, which provides credentials to become a certified technology specialist (a professional who can usually perform general audio-visual technology tasks).

These programs can take several months to up to a year to finish. On-the-job training may include setting up cables or automation systems, testing electrical equipment, learning the codes and standards of the industry, and following safety procedures. Overall employment of broadcast and sound engineering technicians is projected to grow 8 percent from 2016 to 2026, according to the BLS.

WORKING AS A SATELLITE RADIO ENGINEER

Communications technology has made it possible to have satellite radio, such as Sirius XM, broadcasting talk and music via satellite into car radios, home devices, or streaming to laptops, tablets, and smartphones.

A satellite radio engineer may write software to build new and improved broadcast systems. This requires a proficiency with C, C#, and JavaScript programming languages. These engineers need a proven ability to isolate problems in order to debug and validate complex software systems.

The same skills can apply in direct-to-home satellite services, such as DIRECTV and DISH. Those who want to get involved in the technical aspects of developing and maintaining satellites may enter the profession with an electrical or mechanical engineering degree.

In a guide from the Society of Satellite Professionals International, Derek Edinger, head of the engineering group at Space Systems/Loral, which makes next-generation spacecraft and communications systems, said that his company scouts for talent every year at colleges such as Cal Poly, Cornell, MIT, Stanford, and Notre Dame. The satellite industry has steadily grown since 2003, and employers in the field are hungry for talent in engineering, communications, and information technology.

WORKING AS A SPOTIFY COMPUTER CODER

Spotify is a digital music, podcast, and video streaming service that delivers content via the internet and a smartphone app. When you use the service, you stream music or information to your device via an application programming interface (API). The API is the way that people communicate with Spotify.

To make an API, a coder might use Django, a web development framework for Python, specifically made for creating an API. To understand more about APIs, check out the Spotify Web API Tutorial online. The lesson shows how external applications are used to retrieve Spotify content, such as album data and playlists.

Coders at Spotify primarily rely on Python to program its data analysis and other services, but they also code with Java, C, and C++. Spotify is very committed to Python and sponsors conferences and hackathons for Python users. The results of its top-notch coding can be seen in Spotify's personalized playlist services—Discover Weekly and Release Radar.

Spotify programmers write and test lines of code to make sure the applications and software are operating the way they should. Employers usually look to hire those with a bachelor's degree or higher, who have done coursework focusing on programming languages. Companies will always need professional coders, but the Bureau of Labor Statistics predicts that opportunities in the field will slightly decline from 2016 to 2026.

CHAPTER FOUR

FROM PAGE TO SCREEN: COMPUTER SCIENCE IN PUBLISHING

Some media—such as books and magazines—may seem less likely to depend on technology than other forms of media, but in this day and age, nothing escapes the wired hand of technology.

Bill Tipper is a manager of business innovation at a major national bookseller. His job is to promote and sell more books in the digital age. He heads up the editorial team at one of the country's largest booksellers.

To generate interest in books, his team cranks out content that appears on social media such as Twitter, Facebook, and Instagram. He is the executive producer of two podcasts through which authors discuss books. He also oversees company blogs dedicated to different themes—one for science fiction and fantasy, one for teens, and one for parents of younger children. In addition, he edits a blog featuring serious long-form reviews, profiles, and interviews.

Coding and computers have even changed the way we read books. Today, many people will read an entire book on a slender tablet.

To create the blogs, Tipper and his team use WordPress, which offers users complete customization. “I can precisely manipulate WordPress in HTML,” said Tipper, who claimed he has just a small amount of hypertext markup language knowledge. For example, Tipper can take code from his podcasting hosting service and embed it in on a WordPress page so users can see an actual podcast player and access his podcasts through the page.

"An understanding of HTML helps me," said Tipper in an interview for this book. "I know the code that I get from the podcast hosting provider will fit into the piece of content that I'm creating."

Sometimes, Tipper adjusts and uses images for his web content. Although he is not skilled in more advanced programs, such as Photoshop, he has found that the open source image editor called Seashore meets his needs. This software lets Tipper download a book cover image, crop it to the size he wants, create a file size that is appropriate for the web, and upload it the image to the blog's image directory so he can use it.

Tipper, who is completely self-taught with his computer skills, said that many programs like this are available on the Internet, and students can take advantage of tutorials and lessons online to teach themselves how to use these tech tools.

CONTENT IS STILL KING

When it comes to publishing—whether it be books, magazines, newspapers, or online information sites—content is still the driving force. Tipper, like all those in publishing, knows that there will be no audience if the content is weak. His content has to be compelling to keep viewers returning to his blogs and podcasts. Great content keeps the engines of computer-related media humming.

What makes great content? Viewers want originality. They want to read about things and ideas they haven't read before or they will click past. Catchy headlines grab readers and pull them in. Without a good headline, the busy, short-attention span audience clicks to the next thing. People latch on to stories. They want accuracy. Some "hooks" continue to grab viewers—such as lists. These articles have become known as listicles. They are fast to read and often give a quick dose of information that audiences are seeking.

Tipper said that lists ranking an author's work from best to worst can be very popular and give a company's social media team something entertaining and argument provoking to circulate.

READING IN AN E-WORLD

Naturally, technology has changed the way we consume information. Fewer of us read off of printed pages. Growing numbers now read e-books in an electronic format on devices such as the Kindle, iPads, tablets, and even smartphones. Statista .com, which provides statistics and studies from hundreds of thousands of sources, said that in 2018 e-book sales accounted for about a quarter of global book sales, and consumer e-books are projected to generate nearly 20 billion dollars in annual revenue.

Reading published material electronically goes beyond books. As actual sales of printed material decline, magazines and newspapers established a digital presence. The *New York Times, New Yorker, Washington Post*, and almost every other successful publication also publish online.

In addition to text and images, they offer rich media—video, audio, or other elements, that encourage viewers to interact and engage with the content. Some print journalists have had to adapt to become like broadcast journalists, making audio and video segments of the news they cover. In 2017, Bloomberg reported how Mic.com, a news site targeting millennials, revamped its newsroom so that it ended up with sixty-three content providers focused on making digital videos.

Journalists have also found opportunities in information services that have sprung up and thrived on the internet. Many cater to specific niche interests. WebMD and Everyday Health, for example, cater to a public interest in health news. Mental Floss and Boing Boing both feature a quirkier side to the news.

WORKING AS A KINDLE SOFTWARE DESIGNER

The Kindle e-reader team hires software designers who have a background in cutting-edge Java-based web development and exceptional C++ skills. They explore experimental machine learning. Machine learning is a field of computer science that gives computer systems the ability to "learn" with data, without being explicitly programmed. It is part of an overall concept called

The Kindle e-reader has allowed millions of people to hold their libraries literally in the palms of their hands.

artificial intelligence (AI), which is about programming machines to carry out tasks in a way that we would consider "smart."

Kindle designers construct all sorts of Kindle Tools such as Kindle Create, which is a tool consumers can use to transform a completed manuscript into a Kindle e-book. Similarly, Kindle Comic Creator helps users make graphic novels, comics, and manga that can be viewed on a Kindle.

The Bureau of Labor Statistics reports that employment of software developers is projected to grow 24 percent from 2016 to 2026. This is much faster than the average for all occupations. Employment of applications developers is projected to grow 31 percent.

DIGITAL SKILLS FOR WRITERS

Many writers today have to learn about content management systems. Through these software tools, writers can post their work, code headlines to be bold, provide links, and insert various links in their stories. Editors make changes on the content posted on CMS, and the copy can be carefully tracked before it goes to publication.

To deliver strong journalism in the digital age, writers need to plug in to the world of computer technology so they can develop cutting-edge ways to create dynamic content.

In his article "Why Journalists Should Learn Computer Programming" in MediaShift.org, Roland Lybrand said that reporters need more programming skills and knowledge to "tell better and more engaging stories." Columbia University offers Computer Science and Journalism, MIT provides open courseware to learn programming, and the Walleye Foundation offers scholarships for journalists to learn how to code. Reporters who better understand code may also be better equipped to come up with innovative ways to present information and news to the public.

WORKING AS AN INFOGRAPHICS DESIGNER

Infographics are quick, visual methods of delivering information and data in a powerful graphic format. Infographics are designed for the short attention spans of the computer age. They might show the weather or statistical trends. One infographic online displays which members of the Beatles wrote the most hit songs and their Billboard magazine rankings over the years.

Talented infographic designers are hotly sought after in publishing because infographics are popular. An article on the Adobe Blog states that 45 percent more web users will click on a link if it features an infographic or list. Many software tools make creating infographics easier, such as Visme, Infogr.am, and iCharts.

Although there is no set educational path for infographics designers, graphic designer and web designer Matt Morgan writes on the website Infographics Den that online tutorials can help from Planet Photoshop, Udacity, Treehouse, and Absolute Cross. To land jobs, Morgan further recommends building a portfolio with assistance from an online service such as Carbonmade, Dunked, Viewbook, or Behance.

Infographics designers can further sharpen their talents with college classes in art and graphic design. Opportunities for graphic designers are expected to grow between 2016 and 2026 but at a slower rate than average job growth, according to the BLS.

WORKING AS A DESKTOP PUBLISHER

A lot of publishing work today can be farmed out to individuals who have the latest editorial and design skills. Desktop publishers use computer software to design page layouts for newspapers, books, brochures, and other items that are printed or published online, according to the BLS. Adobe InDesign, Microsoft Publisher, and Xara Page & Layout Designer rank among the top software packages used in desktop publishing.

Experience is what counts to get started in this field—some start with just a two-year degree, while others can begin after embarking on short-term on-the-job training for as little as one month. Opportunities are expected to decline, however, as more of these tasks are taken on by editors and designers who work in publishing firms.

WORKING AS A PREPRESS TECHNICIAN

These experts make sure that a publication is properly formatted in terms of appearance and layout of text and images. They may maintain, repair, and troubleshoot presses and printing equipment as needed. Prepress workers often receive digital files of materials to be printed. According to Scholarships

.org, technicians use laser "image setters" to expose digital image pages directly onto the thin metal printing plates or directly to a digital press that can churn out printed pages.

Some get started in the business by earning a two-year associate's degree in prepress skills offered by community colleges, junior colleges, and technical schools. While these technicians are still needed, the BLS says that opportunities are on the decline and may remain so through 2026.

CHAPTER FIVE

REACHING THE MASSES: COMPUTER SCIENCE IN SOCIAL MEDIA

Facebook, Twitter, Instagram. It's hard to remember a time when social media sites like this didn't exist. At their heart, these platforms are intended for people to share personal thoughts and images. Of course, now that social media sites have billions of users, advertisers have been steadily reaching out to people via these channels as well. Online advertising has ballooned into an $88 billion industry.

WORKING AS A DATA ANALYTICS SPECIALIST

One of the appealing things about putting a message out through social media is that response can be measured. Computer technology provides data about how many eyeballs actually saw an advertisement or other message that is posted. After an advertisement has run online, a data analytics specialist can tell how many clicks there were on each ad. Ads are tagged in

With the increased use of social media, such as Facebook, Twitter, and Instagram, data analytics specialists are needed to measure how people use the services.

such a way that it's clear how a customer may have clicked on a specific ad and then come to an online store, for example.

These specialists create effective strategies to collect data, analyze information, conduct research, measure customer response, and implement analytics solutions for products or services, according to Payscale.com. They are familiar with a variety of database software and data analytics software.

A bachelor's degree in analytics, data management, or a related field is generally required for this position.

THE TOP SOCIAL MEDIA SITES

A 2018 poll of 2,002 adults showed who the heavy hitters were in terms of popularity when it came to social media. The numbers here showed the percent of American adults who said they used the following social media sites online or on their phones.

YouTube: 73 percent
Facebook: 68 percent
Instagram: 35 percent
Pinterest: 29 percent
Snapchat: 27 percent
LinkedIn: 25 percent
Twitter: 24 percent

The study noted that Snapchat is an especially big hit with young people. Almost eight out of ten eighteen- to twenty-four-year-olds used Snapchat.

The BLS says that operations research analysts (a related field) will experience a very strong job outlook through 2026.

WORKING AS AN SEO SPECIALIST

To maximize the number of viewers to their websites and pages, companies often hire specialists in search

In the world of the internet, it's all about getting eyeballs on pages. An expert in search engine optimization knows the techniques for getting sites to have the best ranking on search engines.

engine optimization (SEO). Their goal is to maximize online visibility. Search engine traffic can make (or break) an organization's success. Businesses want their pages to show in search engine results pages (SERP), the pages displayed by search engines in response to a query by a searcher.

Bill Tipper worked with a person who was dedicated to this task to help increase book sales. That person's job was to make web pages maximally friendly to search engines. A search engine optimization specialist knows strategies, techniques, and tactics used to increase the amount of visitors. Tipper said:

> **If we are selling a book about Queen Elizabeth II, we want to do everything we can with that page—in terms of its header, keywords, and how the page is set up—so our page comes up in people's searches for Queen Elizabeth II, or the monarchy, or the Crown, or British history.**

One technique for increasing viewers is providing links to relevant related content. While outbound links steer the viewer to some other domain than your site, links to related web content helps search engines understand your product and content. The site Shout Me Loud, which is a popular blog about blogging, said that these links help increase trust and the quality of your site.

The *Search Engine Journal* said that "Every SEO would love to find the magic formula that could once and for all explain how SEO works, with specific rules and concrete equations on the table." Unfortunately, the rules and tactics keep changing. It goes on to say that professionals who handle optimization learn how to combine and experiment with multiple methods and then analyze the results.

Colleges today, such as Cornell College, University of Illinois at Urbana-Champaign, and Temple University, offer degree programs in digital marketing, including lessons on search engine optimization. Overall employment of advertising, promotions, and marketing managers is projected to grow 10 percent from 2016

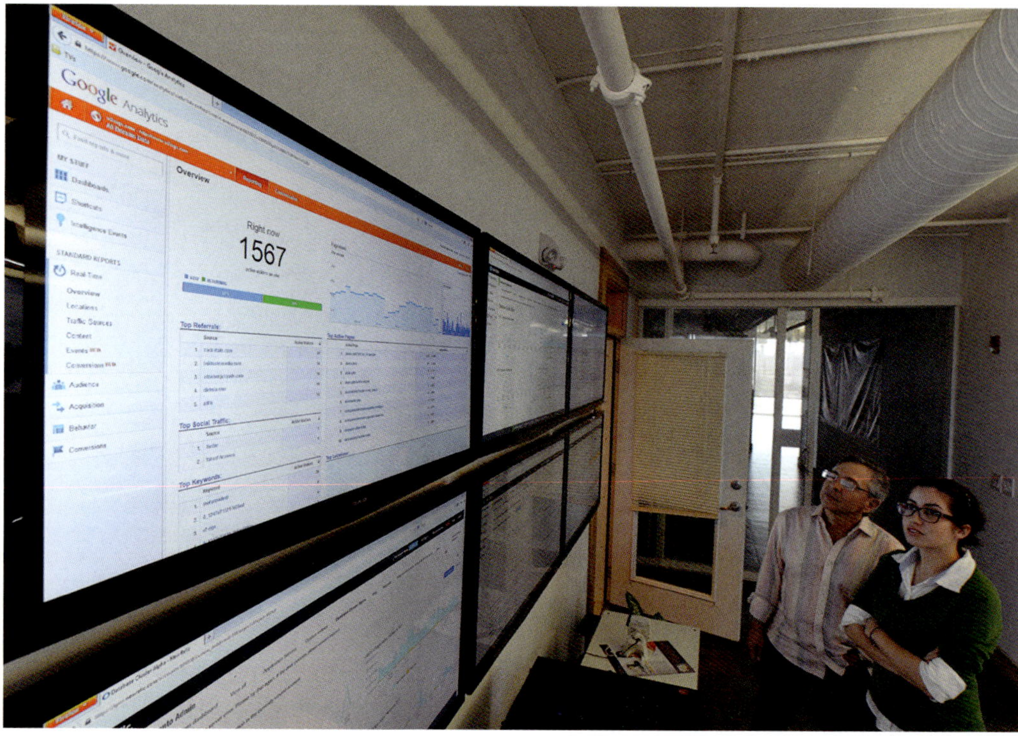

Project coordinators examine real-time Google Analytics data about their firm's website. This type of information can reveal how much attention their product is getting on the internet.

to 2026, faster than the average for all occupations, according to the BLS.

WORKING AS A DIGITAL STRATEGIST

Digital strategist is a related career. These professionals develop and deliver digital marketing plans to a business or a number of clients. They are the experts at engaging consumers on websites—from their own to social media sites. They may help develop online ad campaigns and know how to measure their success.

Digital strategist Megan Zander wrote in *Enterprise Marketer* that collaboration, communication, and organization are key, and computer programs and tools help, such as Jira, Confluence, Slack, Google Docs and Sheets, or GitHub. The digital strategist may take advantage of Google technology that identifies potential customers based on their past searches. With that information, advertisers on Google can target consumers most likely to buy their products.

There is no set educational path for this career but marketing, communications, and computer skills are useful. Some colleges offer programs in internet marketing. The Bureau of Labor Statistics predicts that jobs in marketing management will increase faster than the average through 2026.

BECOME A MASTER OF SOCIAL MEDIA

Most people today are familiar with social media, and young people especially may know their way around Facebook, Twitter, Instagram, Snapchat, LinkedIn, YouTube, Tumblr, and other platforms. Through these online tools, huge numbers of people interact and communicate via computers, smartphones, and tablets.

Big and small companies—from Starbucks to the local neighborhood café—maintain their own pages on social media. Ultimately, their job is to increase sales and profits for the business they work for. They do this by generating content for a company's social channels. The content raises awareness and may drive traffic to a company's site or even motivate people to go to a business's physical location.

This is a creative job that depends on strong writing, graphics skills, and possibly audio and visual design skills. Managers study their target audience and know what they might respond to. They don't necessarily need coding skills, but they do need to know everything about how a social media site works. After they launch a campaign, they know how to use analytic tools to see what the response has been like and to measure its success. Because people often respond and comment on social media posts, these managers often write replies, interacting directly with people online.

As the social media manager for NASA (National Aeronautics and Space Administration), John Yembrick uses all the top social media tools to promote the space program. He generated worldwide attention when he organized a TweetChat between astronaut John Kelly and President Barack Obama. "[With social media], you learn what connects with people," Yembrick said in the book *Getting Paid to Manage Social Media*. "The good thing about social media is you get instant feedback. If you post something and it doesn't do well, you can see that. You have analytics and stats—retweets or shares—you can look at right away."

Similar to a social media manager, an online community manager helps grow a business's online

President Barack Obama, other politicians, and organizations have used social media such as Twitter to get their messages out to the masses.

presence. They are constantly reaching out for ways to widen a company's fan base. The job typically requires writing, sales, marketing, and event-planning experience. A degree in marketing or a related field may also be required.

Several colleges now offer courses specifically designed to train students on using social media in business. For example, Rutgers University has set up a mini-MBA program in social media marketing.

This certificate program helps participants design, manage, and track social media campaigns. At Austin Community College in Texas, students can pursue a two-year program in social media communications. An article from the BLS says that increased use of social media as a way for businesses to communicate with the public indicates ample opportunities for work.

KEEPING UP WITH THE CUTTING EDGE

Media has to be fast to adapt in the computer age. Here are more areas where those with computer knowledge, including programming, are focusing their talents.

STREAMING CONTENT

Streaming media is video or audio content sent in compressed form over the internet and played immediately. In 1992, StarWorks introduced the first commercial streaming product where full action video could be accessed via computer. On September 5, 1995, the world's first live-streaming event occurred when ESPN SportZone streamed a live broadcast of a baseball game between the Seattle Mariners and New York Yankees to listeners via the internet.

Today, consumers are streaming television programs and other media directly to their phones.

Advances in streaming have led to the rise of Netflix, Amazon Video, Hulu, and other similar services. At MIT, computer scientists have constructed an artificial intelligence system that "uses machine learning to pick different algorithms depending on network conditions"—ultimately this creates higher-quality streaming. For those who want to get into the tech side of streaming and learn how to create and enhance streaming through programming, Kitty Gupta recommended learning these languages in an article in Freelancinggig.com: C++, PHP, Java, and JavaScript.

PRIVACY CONTROL

Anyone in media today has to be aware of privacy issues. The Pew Research Center reported that those who access information on the internet have widespread concerns about privacy, and they worry about the ability of businesses to access their personal information. The study also indicated that social media users can feel harassed by a flood of sponsored content directed at them.

The professionals who provide media content and receive information on those who view it have to be sensitive when it comes to using consumer data. Are there legal issues about how much personal data they can gather? This is a concern in the business world and certainly one that a media specialist may have to learn more about. Media companies also have to set up internet protections to block others from hacking into their systems and stealing or corrupting data.

Hackers accessed private emails of movie executives at Sony Pictures in response to its movie *The Interview*. These cybercriminals issued threats to Sony in response to the planned release of the comedy, which was about the assassination of North Korean leader Kim Jong-un. Hackers have also been able to rob companies of sensitive subscriber information, such as credit card numbers and Social Security numbers. Internet security specialists work to prevent these kinds of web crimes.

Some colleges offer courses specific to cybersecurity, including security technologies and enforcement, statistical analysis of cyberattacks, web technologies, cryptography, and legal issues. High school students interested in this topic may want to check out Hacker High School, which promotes security awareness for teens. Hacker High School provides a set of hands-on lessons designed specifically for teens to learn about cybersecurity and gain some critical internet skills. Programming languages used in computer security include C++, Java, Python, Lisp, and Perl.

VIRTUAL REALITY

For anyone in media, keeping up with the newest technology can advance a career. Virtual reality (VR) creates a 3D computer-generated 360-degree environment that immerses viewers in another world.

The future of journalism may involve documenting news stories so they can be viewed in a 360-degree simulated environment using virtual-reality headsets.

Several companies produce VR technology, including Unity 3D, IrisVR, and Oculus VR. As the technology advances and becomes more popular, journalists are envisioning it as a way to heighten storytelling and create a new form of immersive journalism.

NPR journalist Barbara Allen came up with the idea to simulate the aftermath of Hurricane Katrina using VR. Collaborating with Stanford University's Virtual Human Interaction Lab, she helped produce a VR experience of the disaster where viewers saw the waters rising around them, heard cries for help in the distance, and watched helicopters flying overhead.

Many media organizations, such as the *New York Times*, *Wall Street Journal*, Vice, PBS, and *The Guardian* are exploring using VR more to share stories. Virtual reality technology may grow to be a medium that is popularly used to distribute information, news, and television programs.

When it comes to finding challenging and rewarding work in the media industry, always keep your computer skills sharp, and always continue to learn and remain curious about how computer technology works.

GLOSSARY

actualities Recorded audio segments from a news scene, containing the voice or voices of the newsmaker or interview subject.

algorithm A step-by-step procedure for solving a problem. A computer program is an elaborate algorithm.

analytics The discovery and interpretation of meaningful patterns in data.

Android A smartphone operating system developed by Google.

blog A regularly updated website or web page that is written in an informal or conversational style. Often blogs are run by an individual or small group but larger organizations and companies have blogs as well.

broadband High-speed, high-capacity data transmission through a single cable.

cloud-based services Applications and other products accessed on demand through the internet from a provider's servers.

cryptography The science of code making and code breaking.

cybersecurity Protecting internet-connected systems, including hardware, software, and data, from cyberattacks.

hackathon An event, often lasting several days, in which a large number of people meet to engage in collaborative computer programming.

hacker An expert of computer systems and programming languages who typically knows how to gain unauthorized access to computers systems.

hosting service In general, a computer that is set up to offer services to customers. Clients connect to the hosting service via the internet.

HTML (Hypertext Markup Language) The computer coding language used to create web pages. HTML provides instructions about a web page's format and what is to be displayed on the page.

machine learning A branch of artificial intelligence that is based on the idea that computers can learn and make decisions from data and patterns.

podcast Typically, a series of downloadable audio files (although sometimes in video format) that provide content for audiences that can be listened to on portable devices or home computers.

rich media A digital advertising term for an ad that includes sophisticated features like video, audio, and streaming.

search engine optimization (SEO) The process of using tech skills to maximize the number of visitors to a website. SEO raises a website higher on the list of results returned by a search engine.

server In the internet world, servers are dedicated computers that store web page information and then serve (or deliver) it to the user.

social media Networks and related computer-based tools used to create and share content and participate in social networking. Facebook, Twitter, and Instagram are all examples of social media.

software Programs used to operate computers.

tablet A portable computer, usually smaller than a laptop, that operates primarily via a touchscreen.

transcribe To make a written copy, often from recorded material.

virtual reality A 360-degree environment that is simulated by a computer but which fully immerses the viewer with sights, sounds, and sometimes touch.

wav file An audio file format for recording and storing uncompressed audio data.

Canadian Advanced Technology Alliance (CATA)
207 Bank Street, Suite 416
Ottawa, ON K2P 2N2
Canada
(613) 236-6550
Website: http://www.cata.ca
Twitter: @CATAAlliance
The largest high-tech association in Canada, CATA is a comprehensive resource of the latest high-tech news in Canada.

CompTIA Association of Information Technology Professionals (AITP)
1500 Lacey Road
Downers Grove, IL 60515
Website: http://www.aitp.org
(866) 835-8020
Twitter: @CompTIAAITP
This worldwide society of professionals in information technology offers career training, scholarships, news, and social networking opportunities.

MediaSmarts
950 Gladstone Avenue, Suite 120
Ottawa, ON K1Y 3E6
Canada
(613) 224-7721
Website: http://mediasmarts.ca
Facebook and Twitter: @MediaSmarts
This Canadian not-for-profit organization for digital

and media literacy has helpful resources on these subjects. MediaSmarts' work falls into the areas of education, public awareness, research, and policy.

National Association of Programmers
PO Box 529
Prairieville, LA 70769
Website: http://www.napusa.org
This group is dedicated to providing information and resources to help programmers, developers, consultants, and students in the computer industry.

OpenMedia
1424 Commercial Drive
PO Box 21674
Vancouver, BC V5L 5G3
Canada
(604) 633-2744
Website: http://openmedia.ca
Facebook: @openmediaorg
Twitter: @OpenMedia_ca
OpenMedia is a Canadian grassroots organization that safeguards the possibilities of the open and affordable internet.

TryComputing.org
445 Hoes Lane
Piscataway, NJ 08854-4141
(732) 981-0060
Website: http://www.trycomputing.org/inspire/computing-student-opportunities

This site from the Institute of Electrical and Electronics Engineers features competitions, events, internships, and research programs for young people. You can also find out about career opportunities and colleges with computer programming courses.

FOR FURTHER READING

Bedell, Jane. *So, You Want to Be a Coder?* New York: Alladin/Simon & Schuster, 2016.

Culver, Sherri Hope. *Media Career Guide: Preparing for Jobs in the 21st Century*. New York, NY: Bedford/St. Martin's, 2018.

Kawasaki, Guy and Peg Fitzpatrick. *The Art of Social Media: Power Tips for Power Users*. New York, NY: Portfolio, 2014.

McCue, Camille. *Coding for Kids for Dummies*. Hoboken, NJ: Wiley, 2014.

Mueller, John Paul. *Artificial Intelligence for Dummies*. Hoboken, NJ: Wiley, 2018.

Rauf, Don. *Getting Paid to Manage Social Media*. New York, NY: Rosen Publishing, 2017.

Roberts, Lauren. *Careers in Digital Media*. San Diego, CA: Reference Point Press, 2017.

Smith, Stephanie. *Careers in Media and Communication*. Thousand Oaks, CA: SAGE Publications, 2018.

Vanden-Heuvel, John C. *Web Design for Kid*s. New York, NY: Little Bee Books, 2016.

Wainewright, Max. *How to Code: A Step-By-Step Guide to Computer Coding.* Asheville, NC: Sterling Children's Books, 2016.

Woodcock, Jon, and Kiki Prottsman. *Star Wars Coding Project*s. New York, NY: DK Publishing, 2017.

BIBLIOGRAPHY

Ballenson, Jeremy. "How Virtual Reality Could Change the Journalism Industry." *PBS NewsHour*, January 15, 2018. https://www.pbs.org/newshour/economy/making-sense/how-virtual-reality-could-change-the-journalism-industry.

Bindrim, Kira. "It's Time to Get Over Yourself and Start Reading Books on Your iPhone." Quartz, January 10, 2017. https://qz.com/880425/reading-books-on-your-smartphone-is-bad-for-the-eyes-but-good-for-the-brain.

Deprogrammed Radio World. "Broadcasting Vs. Podcasting: What Is the Difference?" Retrieved September 5, 2018. https://www.deprogrammedradio.com/making-your-own-programs-for-free/item/256-broadcasting-vs-podcasting-what-is-the-difference.

Elgan, Mike. "Kids Can't Compute—And That's a Problem." *Forbes*, November 14, 2013. https://www.forbes.com/sites/netapp/2013/11/14/kids-cant-compute-problem/#4fc5650131d1.

Elrick, Lauren. "What Does a Software Developer Do? A Behind-the-Scenes Look." Rasmussen College, November 21, 2016. https://www.rasmussen.edu/degrees/technology/blog/what-does-software-developer-do.

Grossman, Joan. Phone interview with the author on August 28, 2018.

Halbrooks, Glenn. "Pros and Cons of Working in the Media Industry." The Balance Careers, May 2, 2018. https://www.thebalancecareers.com/the-pros-and-cons-of-careers-in-the-media-industry-2315118.

Hiemstra, Mark John. "What You Need to Know About the Future of Video Streaming." HaiVision: Video at Work, December 20, 2017. https://www.haivision.com/blog/live-video-streaming/future-video-streaming-technology.

Jacobs, Fred. "Broadcasting and Podcasting." Jacobs Media Strategies, August 21, 2017 https://jacobsmedia.com/broadcasting-podcasting-podcasting-broadcasting.

Levy, Jon. "Everything You Need to Know to Start Your Own Podcast, According to the Pros." *Forbes*, February 28, 2018. https://www.forbes.com/sites/jonlevy/2018/02/28/everything-you-need-to-know-to-start-your-own-podcast-according-to-the-pros/#61f527a6792e.

MacAdam, Allison. "What Does a Radio Script Look Like?" NPR Training, March 9, 2015. https://training.npr.org/audio/what-does-a-radio-script-look-like.

Medium. "How Has the Media Changed in the Past 10 Years? We Ask the Experts." Originally published on Digital Innovators Summit Blog, September 9, 2016. https://medium.com/@DISummit/how-has-the-media-changed-in-the-past-10-years-we-ask-the-experts-cc4df1ebd9cd.

Morgan, Matt. "How to Become an Infographic Designer." December 20, 2017. https://infographicden.co.uk/infographics-blog/become-infographic-designer.

PC Magazine. "Data Analytics." Retrieved October 2, 2018. https://www.pcmag.com/business/directory/data-analytics.

Rosenblum, Michael. Email interview with the author.

Sinclair, Hannah. "Should Journalists Learn How to Code? It Can't Hurt." Medium, July 17, 2017. https://medium.com/the-walkley-magazine/should-journalists-learn-how-to-code-it-cant-hurt-ef04ce327fe4.

Smith, Aaron, and Monica Anderson. "Social Media Use in 2018." Pew Research Center, March 1, 2018. http://www.pewinternet.org/2018/03/01/social-media-use-in-2018.

Smith, Gerry. "Publishers Are Making More Video—Whether You Want It or Not." Bloomberg, August 29, 2017. https://www.bloomberg.com/news/articles/2017-08-29/publishers-are-making-more-video-whether-you-want-it-or-not.

University of Sheffield. "Lets Podcast. Retrieved September 5, 2018. https://www.sheffield.ac.uk/letspodcast/intro.

WDD Staff. "A Brief History of Blogging." Web Design Depot, March 14, 2011. https://www.webdesignerdepot.com/2011/03/a-brief-history-of-blogging.

Zambelli, Alex. "A History of Media Streaming and the Future of Connected TV." March 1, 2013. https://www.theguardian.com/media-network/media-network-blog/2013/mar/01/history-streaming-future-connected-tv.

Zander, Megan. "What Does a Digital Strategist Do?" *Enterprise Marketer*, January 3, 2017. https://enterprisemarketer.com/articles/digital-marketing-nerd.

INDEX

H

I

J

K

L

M

N

O

P

R

S

ABOUT THE AUTHOR

Don Rauf is the author of multiple nonfiction books, including *Killer Lipstick and Other Spy Gadgets; A Teen's Guide to the Power of Social Networking,* and *Getting the Most Out of Makerspaces to Explore Arduino and Electronics.* He lives in Seattle.

PHOTO CREDITS

Cover Westend61/Getty Images; back cover, pp. 4–5 (background) nadla/E+/Getty Images; p. 5 (inset) tetxu /Shutterstock.com; pp. 8, 20, 30, 42, 53 (background) VLADGRIN/Shutterstock.com, (circuit pattern) Titima Ongkantong/Shutterstock.com; p. 9 Starikov Pavel /Shutterstock.com; p. 11 NurPhoto/Getty Images; p. 15 Twinsterphoto/Shutterstock.com; p. 17 Joe Amon /The Denver Post/Getty Images; p. 21 Barcroft Media /Getty Images; p. 23 Courtesy of Roku, Inc.; p. 25 Sharaf Maksumov/Shutterstock.com; p. 27 Adrian Dennis/AFP/Getty Images; p. 31 Boston Globe/Getty Images; p. 32 Guitarist Magazine/Getty Images; p. 36 Courtesy Avid Technology, Inc.; p. 38 MichaelJayBerlin /Shutterstock.com; p. 43 Andrey_Popov/Shutterstock .com; p. 46 Davide Zanchetta/Shutterstock.com; p. 49 Alexandros Michailidis/Shutterstock.com; p. 54 BigTunaOnline/Shutterstock.com; p. 56 © iStockphoto .com/PeopleImages; p. 58 Bloomberg/Getty Images; p. 61 Mandel Ngan/AFP/Getty Images; p. 65 Odd Andersen/AFP/Getty Images; additional background textures and graphics Verticalarray/Shutterstock.com (p. 1), Toria/Shutterstock.com (p. 3).

Design: Michael Moy; Layout: Nicole Russo-Duca; Photo Research: Nicole DiMella